D0288521

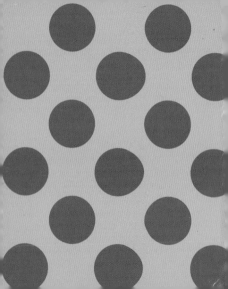

MOM

RUNNING PRESS
PHILADELPHIA · LONDON

Library of Congress Cataloging-in-Publication Number 96-69235
ISBN 0-7624-0039-0

This book may be ordered by mail from the publisher.
Please include $1.00 for postage and handling.
But try your bookstore first!

Running Press Book Publishers
125 South Twenty-second Street
Philadelphia, Pennsylvania 19103-4399

CONTENTS

INTRODUCTION

*T*hroughout history moms have been applauded for their ability to perform many different roles. Some moms are cab drivers: "I'll pick you up at five." Others are referees: "One hour without TV for hitting your brother." Still others fashion consultants: "Don't forget your raincoat." Or great compromisers: "Tonight's special is meatloaf or meatloaf. Which can I interest you in?"

Moms deliver their lines with laughter, smiles, or a straight face. But they always have a twinkle in their eye because they know they're responsible for the well-being of their children. Whether they are burping a three-month baby, wrestling with a two-year old who wants to put glue in her hair, or comforting a six-year-old boy who didn't make the team, moms always know just what to say.

With their wonderful knowledge and insight into the hearts of their babies—whether two months old or twenty-six—moms have all the answers. But they know the best answer is usually just a smile and a hug. Because that's what moms do best. Forget the applause—moms can take home all the trophies and awards there are, but the biggest reward is always love of their children.

Inside this book are quotes from moms, dads, children, and grandchildren celebrating motherhood in the way moms appreciate the most—with love.

Our
MOTHERS

My first vivid memory is . . .
when first I looked into her face
and she looked into mine. That I do
remember, and that exchanging look
I have carried with me all my life.
We recognized each other. I was her
child and she was my mother. . . .

Pearl S. Buck (1892–1973)
American writer

My mother is my root, my foundation. She planted the seed that I base my life on, and that is the belief that the ability to achieve starts in your mind.

Michael Jordan (b. 1963)
American athlete

I say: "Mommy? Will you come be with me?" When she came to Australia with me, I think I got sick purposely. I think my system just knew it was safe to get sick and let my mom totally take care of me and bring me tea.

Alicia Silverstone (b. 1976)
American actress

My mother is
my mirror and
I am hers.
What do we see?
Our face grown
young again...

Marge Piercy (b. 1936)
American writer

18

*T*o my mother I tell **the** truth. I have no thought, **no** feeling that I cannot share with **my** mother, and she is like a second co**ns**cience to me, her eyes like a mirror **ref**lecting my own image.

William Gerhardi (1895-1977)
American writer

My mother wanted me to be her wings, to fly as she never quite had the courage to do. I love her for that. I love the fact that she wanted to give birth to her own wings.

Erica Jong (b. 1942)
American writer and poet

*T*he doctors told me that
I would never walk,
but my mother told me I would,
so I believed my mother.

Wilma Rudolph (b. 1940)
American athlete

She made me a security blanket when I was born. That faded green blanket lasted just long enough for me to realize that the security part came from her.

Alexander Cane
20th-century American writer

My mother was the most beautiful woman…. All I am I owe to my mother…. I attribute all my success in life to the moral, intellectual and physical education I received from her.

George Washington (1732–1799)
American President

As a child you never quite understood how your mom was able to know exactly what you were thinking. . . . Sometimes Mom would know what you were thinking before the thought entered your head. "Don't even think about punching your brother," she would warn before you had time to make a fist.

Linda Sunshine
20th-century American writer

My mother's great. She has the major looks. She could stop you from doing anything, through a closed door even, with a single look. Without saying a word, she has that power to rip out your tonsils.

Whoopi Goldberg (b. 1949)
American actress and comedian

One time I ran out of the store
and took the bus home by myself
after my mother asked a salesclerk
where the "underpants" counter
was. Everyone in the store heard her.
I had no choice.

Phyllis Theroux
20th-century American writer

I wanted to run away from home, but my mother would kill me if I went out on the highway before they put a traffic light in.

I don't want to be a mother. Ever.

Laura Parsons
American schoolgirl, age 11

We never make sport of religion, politics, race, or mothers. A mother never gets hit with a custard pie. Mothers-in-law, yes. But mothers—never.

**Mack Sennett (1884–1960)
American movie director**

Mommy looked at me, her eyes squinched up in laughter, a grin spreading across her face. She loves for me to mess with her, gets a big kick out of my

tongue-in-cheek
assaults on her dignity.
As if anything could
ever put a dent in
her dignity.

Bebe Moore Campbell (b. 1950)
American writer

*M*om didn't do anything very exciting with her life except bask in her sons' success. But I never got the feeling she sacrificed herself for us—whatever she gave she found her own quiet pleasure in.

Neil Simon (b. 1927)
American playwright

Time is the judge. If you manage
to pass on what you have to the
next generation, then what you did
was right.

Barbara Kingsolver (b. 1955)
American writer

There shall never be another quite so tender, quite so kind as the patient little mother, nowhere on this earth you'll find her affection duplicated. . . .

Paul C. Brownlow
20th-century writer

Fifty-four years of love and tenderness and crossness and devotion and unswerving loyalty. Without her I could have achieved a quarter of what I have achieved, not only in terms of success and career, but in terms of personal happiness. . . . She has never stood between me and my life, never tried to hold me too tightly, always let me go free. . . .

Noël Coward (1899–1973)
English playwright and actor

It was my mother who gave me my voice. She did this, I know now, by clearing a space where my words could fall, grow, then find their way to others.

Paula Giddings (b. 1948)
American writer

My mother's love for me
was so great that I have
worked hard to justify it.

Marc Chagall (1887–1985)
Russian-born French artist

*M*y mother always joked that my first word was "Mine." Needless to say, my memory couldn't help me, but I do remember years later, looking at her for what seemed the first time, and saying it again.

Madison Riley
20th-century American writer

A greeting card sent by a 25-year-old son to his mother half a continent away reads: "Mom, you asked me in kindergarten, you asked me in grade school, you asked me in junior high, you asked me in high school, you asked me in college, you asked me after college, and I finally know what I want to be: A KID!"

Zenith Henkin Gross
20th-century American journalist

In my interest she
left no wire unpulled,
no stone unturned,
no cutlet uncooked.

Winston Churchill (1874–1965)
English statesman and writer

You're a great mum and I love you. I'm outta here.

Michael Boyd, son of Julia Boyd

Our

CHILDREN

People who say they
sleep like a baby usu-
ally don't have one.

L. J. Burke

There was never a child so lovely but his mother was glad to get him asleep.

Ralph Waldo Emerson (1803–1882)
American essayist and poet

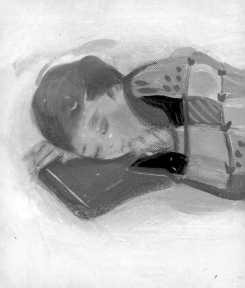

The commonest fallacy among women is that simply having children makes one a mother—which is as absurd as believing that having a piano makes one a musician.

Sydney J. Harris (1917-1986)
American writer

If you bungle raising your children, I don't think whatever else you do well matters very much.

Jacqueline Kennedy Onassis (1929-1994)
American editor and First Lady

In a child's lunch box,
a mother's thoughts.

Japanese proverb

At the moment that a boy of 13 is turning toward girls, a girl of 13 is turning on her mother. This girl can get rather unreasonable, often saying such comical things as "Listen, this is my life!"

Bill Cosby (b. 1937)
American comedian, writer, and actor

People always talked about a mother's uncanny ability to read her children, but that was nothing compared to how children could read their mothers.

Anne Tyler (b. 1941)
American writer

My friend horrified me with the tale that her three-year-old wouldn't "let" her play any of her own tapes. Yes, Mozart and Bach are taboo chez this child. Mother must play the three-year-old's tapes—or face the consequences, i.e. high-pitched whining, deafening volume, boring repetition of the same flat phrase. Well, sometimes those tapes themselves carry similar consequences.

Sonia Taitz
20th-century American writer

Children seldom
misquote you.
They more often
repeat word for word
what you shouldn't
have said.

Mae Maloo

What the daughter does,
the mother did.

Jewish proverb

I spent my summer the same way I spent my winter. I'm a mini-mom. When my mom is away at work I take care of my younger brother and three sisters. . . .

I put them to bed when they're not sleepy.

And when they follow their "real mother," I grab them around the neck and hold on tight until they turn purple.

There is a lot of hitting and spitting with the job.

Laura Parsons
American schoolgirl, age 11

A daughter reminds you of all the things you had forgotten about being young. Good and bad.

Maeve O'Reilly

They always say that children are a joy. But at times they can be the most appalling headaches.

Rosamunde Pilcher (b. 1924)
English writer

"I know one thing," she said hoarsely. "I know that if there is an afterlife, I'm going to have a very different kind of family. I'm going to have nothing but fabulously rich, witty, and enchanting children."

John Cheever (1912–1982)
American writer

Thank God
kids never mean well.

Lily Tomlin (b. 1939)
American actress and comedian

Never lend your car
to anyone to whom
you have given birth.

Erma Bombeck (1927–1996)
American writer

A vacation frequently means that the family goes away for a rest, accompanied by a mother who sees that they all get it.

Marcelene Cox

A suburban mother's role is to deliver children obstetrically once, and by car ever after.

Peter De Vries (1910–1993)
American writer

Life ... would give her everything
of consequence, life would shape her,
not we. All we were good for was
to make the introductions.

Helen Hayes (1900–1993)
American actress

The trouble with cleaning
the house is that it gets
dirty the next day anyway.
So, skip a week if you
have to. The children are
the most important thing.

Barbara Bush (b. 1925)
American First Lady

Every breath she ever breathed, every effort she ever made, every prayer she ever prayed was for her son. . . . The greatest break that Francis Albert Sinatra ever enjoyed in his entire life, in his entire career, was to have Dolly as a mother.

Robert Perella

My mother sang with me in her stomach; I sang with Bobbi Kris in my stomach. I believe the child starts to develop within, and whatever is put inside of you—whatever you read, whatever you think, whatever you do—affects the child.

Whitney Houston (b. 1963)
American singer

I am an onlooker on my daughter's dance, which I . . . made possible because she came through me . . . I'm not a part of her dance. Yet whenever she takes a pause and needs someone to talk to, I am there. But that special dance with the child and the future is hers.

Liv Ullman (b. 1939)
Norwegian actress and writer

A mother is not a person
to lean on but a person to
make leaning unnecessary.

Dorothy Canfield Fisher (1879–1958)
American writer

Children are likely
to live up to what you
believe of them.

Lady Bird Johnson (b. 1912)
American First Lady

OURSELVES

When you have your own children, they're part you and part not-you, and then they get away from you and part of you goes with them. But you have to try to remember that part of you that's you and not them. That way, you can let them go.

Bobbie Ann Mason (b. 1940)
American writer

Oh what a power is mother-hood, Possessing a potent spell.

Euripides (484—406 B.C.)
Greek playwright

Making the decision to have a child—it's momentous. It is to decide forever to have your heart go walking around outside your body.

Elizabeth Stone
20th-century American writer

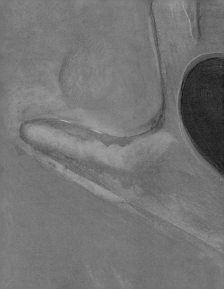

I always say, "You show me a woman with 15 children, and I'll show you an overbearing woman."

Phyllis Diller (b. 1917)
American comedian and writer

*If you want to know
what it feels like to have
a baby—grab hold
of your lower lip.
Now—pull it over the
back of your head!*

**Carol Burnett (b. 1936)
American actress and comedian**

I've heard so many females say
that they became mothers because
they wanted to feel like women, as
if they felt like longshoremen at
all other times.

Bill Cosby (b. 1937)
American actor, comedian, and writer

*M*otherhood is like
Albania—you can't
trust the brochures, you have to
go there.

Marni Jackson
20th-century American journalist

LOVE
MOM

Holding your firstborn, your wife looks at you through different eyes, a traveler from another country. The mothering cues are clearly rooted very deep in the female psyche.

Charlton Heston (b. 1924)
American actor

*I*n the sheltered simplicity of the first days after a baby is born, one sees again the magical closed circle, the miraculous sense of two people existing only for each other.

Anne Morrow Lindbergh (b. 1906)
American writer and aviator

Motherhood cannot finally be delegated. Breast-feeding may succumb to the bottle; cuddling, fondling, and pediatric visits may also be done by fathers (and surely we could make life easier for mothers than we do), but when a child needs a mother to talk to, nobody else but a mother will do.

Erica Jong (b. 1942)
American writer and poet

There is no division nor subtraction in the heart-arithmetic of a good mother. There are only addition and multiplication.

Bess Street Aldrich
20th-century American writer

Every beetle is a gazelle in the eyes of its mother.

Moorish proverb

Every mother is like Moses. She does not enter the promised land. She prepares a world she will not see.

Paul VI [Giovanni Battista] (1897–1978)
Italian-born pope

Life takes surprising turns. The only sure thing is that no parent, ever, has turned out to be perfectly wise and exhaustively provident 1,440 minutes a day, for 18 years.

Barbara Kingsolver (b. 1955)
American writer

I wouldn't have had kids if I thought I had to be perfect for them.

Lucy Ferriss (b. 1954)
American writer

Everyone asks how I find the time
for all the things I do. I make the
time. Being a mother and a wife is
always demanding.

Florence Griffith Joyner (1959–1998)
American athlete

I did it [raised my children] ad hoc, like any working woman does. Every woman who's got a household knows exactly what I did. I did it on a minute-to-minute basis.... There was

never a place I worked,
or a time I worked,
that my children did
not interrupt me, no
matter how trivial—
because it was never
trivial to them.

Toni Morrison (b. 1931)
American writer

Ask your child what he wants for dinner only if he's buying.

Fran Lebowitz (b. 1951)
American writer

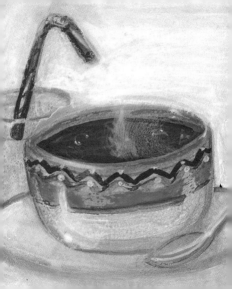

As a housewife, I feel that if the kids are still alive when my husband gets home from work, then, I've done my job.

Roseanne (b. 1953)
American comedian and actress

I've always blamed my
shortcomings as a mother
on the fact that I studied Child
Psychology and Discipline under
an unmarried professor whose only
experience was in raising a dog.
He obviously saw little difference.

Erma Bombeck (1927–1996)
American writer

In God's great vaudeville,
Mother is the headliner.

Elbert Hubbard (1856–1915)
American writer

Lifesaving techniques are, in themselves, a wonderful idea. What makes some of the safety entrepreneurs notorious, however, is the pressure they put on mothers to take their courses and, once within the course, to feel blood terror over every possible life contingency.

Sonia Taitz
20th-century American writer

As a parent you try to maintain a certain amount of control and so you have this tug-of-war.... You have to learn when to let go. And that's not easy.

Aretha Franklin (b. 1942)
American singer

There came a moment quite suddenly a mother realized that a child was no longer hers. . . . Without bothering to ask or even give notice, her daughter had just grown up.

Alice Hoffman (b. 1952)
American writer

The mother-child relationship is paradoxical and, in a sense, tragic. It requires the most intense love on the mother's side, yet this very love must help the child grow away from the mother and become fully independent.

Erich Fromm (1900–1980)
American psychoanalyst

If you want to know
who the real heroes of
world history are, just
look at the mothers.

Peter Høeg (b. 1957)
Danish writer

*A*t work you think of the children you've left at home. At home, you think of the work you've left unfinished. Such a struggle is unleashed within yourself; your heart is rent.

Golda Meir (1898–1978)
Israeli politician

It's the three pairs of
eyes that mothers have
to have. . . . One pair
that see through closed
doors. Another in the
back of her head . . .
and, of course, the
ones in front that can

look at a child when
he goofs up and reflect
"I understand and I
love you" without so
much as uttering a
word.

Erma Bombeck (1927–1996)
American writer

I dig being a mother. . . .

Whoopi Goldberg (b. 1949)
American actress and comedian

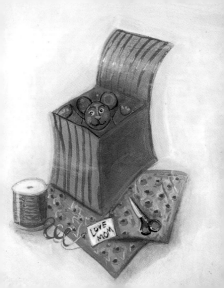

This book has been bound using handcrafted methods, and Smyth-sewn to ensure durability.

The dust jacket and interior were designed by Corinda Cook.

The dust jacket was illustrated by Dan Yaccarino.

The interior was illustrated by Deborah Healy.

The text was edited by Virginia Mattingly.

The text was set in BeLucian, Bureau Eagle, and Shelley Andante Script.